COMING FULL CIRCLE:

BY: Dr. Veter Nichols

ISBN-13:978-0692424100
ISBN-10: 0692424105

Unless otherwise indicated, all scripture quotations contained within are taken from the Thomas Nelson King James Version of the Bible 2003 and Bible Plus 2005. The Zondervan Amplified Version 1987 is noted by AV. Reproduction of the information contained within is forbidden unless prior permission is obtain from the copyright claimants.

COMING FULL CIRCLE

By Prophetess Veter Nichols

DR. VETER NICHOLS

TABLE OF CONTENTS

Foreword

When mom asked us to write the foreword for this book, we were shocked and flattered at the same time. The weight of the task was heavy, not because we didn't know what to say, but it was such a profound honor and we didn't want to take it lightly. Honestly, she could have asked anybody with more influence and status, but she chose us. Besides, who knows and loves her more than us — besides God? No one.

We can't begin to say how proud we are of our mother. We have seen her go through and overcome so many obstacles and battles — physically, mentally, emotionally, and spiritually. Yet, through it all, she always rises to the top like a champion. People only know her by what they see, but we've had the privilege firsthand of knowing her for who she truly is.

In this book, she's not telling you something she hasn't lived out in her own life, but she's sharing a part of her story and journey. As her daughters, we can say, for real, that she is a TRUE woman of God. Not perfect, but perfect in Him. She walks out what she preaches and teaches every day.

Life hasn't always been easy, especially, following the loss of her loving husband of forty years, and our father, William T. Nichols. She could have given up on life, and she almost did, but she battled through sickness and near death to continue to do the will of God, because that wasn't the end of her story.

She's "coming full circle." We've seen our mother undergo a metamorphosis and watched God restore her youth. Truly, she looks as young as we do. She's beginning again and we are so godly-proud of her for having the faith, tenacity, and fortitude to keep fighting. She's a true finisher and we know she will finish empty. We pray God will continue to give her the strength to give, share, birth out, impact, and reach every life that God has entrusted and will entrust to her care.

At the end of the day she's not just our mom, she's our hero. She's a woman of class, strength, and courage. She's an example of who we aspire to be, and we hope this book will encourage each of you in your journey of faith to stay in the fight no matter what it looks like.

We love you mom, more than words can express. You are our friend and we thank you for giving us the opportunity to share just a glimpse of who you are to us with the rest of world.

All our love,

Cherise "TC" Nichols Jackson

Bridgette Nichols Brooks

SECTION I

PREDESTINATION

In the beginning, when God created the heavens and the earth, the earth was formless, and darkness was upon the face of the deep; God had an ultimate plan. Despite the apparent void, God knew exactly what he had in mind—likewise, our lives may appear to be in present darkness and chaos, but in accordance to Jeremiah 29:11, God has a predestined plan for each of us with a specific result. In short, we are becoming who we already were in the heart of God even before we were conceived and formed in our mother's womb

"For I know the plans I have for you," declares the Lord, "plans to prosper you and not to harm you, plans to give you a hope and a future." (Jeremiah 29:11 NIV)

We are bound for this place of perfection, completeness and wholeness in Christ. We were born with purpose already in us. In fact, before we were born, God created and deposited purpose in us. Before the foundation of the world, and prior to being placed into our father's loins, and the seed incubated in our mother's womb, our purpose and origins were already birthed in the heart of God. Before our physical bodies even made an appearance in the natural realm, there was a sure word spoken declaring purpose to our existence. As we become more acquainted with our Creator, He begins to draw out the deposit of himself that he placed in us before TIME was formed; in other words, when He calls to Himself in us, our true purpose begins to blossom.

I realize I didn't just come to this earth at the will of my parents. I manifested in the earth's realm because I was in the Father's heart and mind from the beginning before the foundation of the world. I was supposed to be here at this time. I could not have come any sooner or later, but I came in my predestined time. I'm becoming what I was and the person I was meant to be—that is, becoming what the "I AM" called me to be and living out that predestined purpose.

We must apprehend that which apprehended us. A square peg into a round hole is totally impossible. You can't change who you are or who you were predestined to be. You cannot fit into a mold of something that you were not created to be because God foreordained everything in a particular way, and to occur at a precise time. He ordained a divine order by which everything flows, known as the process of life.

The PROCESS OF LIFE is necessary and inevitable. In order to truly become whom God planned, you will have to go through the process. It develops the understanding, maturity, and character that is necessary to fulfill your God-given purpose. One of the biggest challenges we'll always have to face and overcome throughout this process is fear. To overcome fear, you must deal with the pain and opposition that comes with it in order to get to your true purpose. This understanding of life will lead you to embrace and accept the challenges without backtracking in doubt—you will become completely who you were born to be. When you stop running from your fears and confront them head on your life will forever change.

I have always said, and I believe that your purpose protects you. When you are truly seeking God's divine destiny for your life and walking in it, your life cannot end until you fulfill that purpose. Therefore, it is vital that you face and conquer your greatest fear—the *primary* thing that you continuously run away from keeps you from your potential for greatness and success. Some of us fear success more than failure because so much more responsibility is required to attain success. However, God didn't design us to fail; like Joseph, he wants to give us favor and success in everything we do, when we place Him in total control in our lives.

We all must conquer our greatest fears that will absolutely interrupt God's divine flow. Our fears infringe upon the movement of God and His timing in the realm of the spirit. So I believe this book, "Coming Full Circle," is a tool that can help believers learn how to identify their fears and deal with them in order to fulfill the divine call for which he or she was born.

Your enemy and the adversities of life can be the vehicle that pushes you into your Destiny. The greater your opposition—the greater your reward. Until you conquer your Goliath, you cannot experience the magnitude of the reward that God predetermined for you to have and walk in. The greatest push will be experienced in the realm of the spirit when you face your greatest fear or greatest adversary—rejection, hurt and pain—to actually become who you were born to be and walk in what the Lord has ordained for your life.

The pain associated with the process is a part of making us and unlocking our destiny. God has a predestined plan that will never change for each one of us, because God doesn't change his mind and he cannot lie. Whatever he established is forever.

The Bible tells us that before the foundation of the world, God had predestined us to be holy. So, He is certainly calling for a holy people that can fulfill His call for the Kingdom. In order to fulfill that mission, and come to the place where you want and desire to achieve God's mandate, you must first learn to win at every stage of the process. You must yield to the purpose, regardless of what you've got to go through to get there. So, get started and get moving. In order to start, we need to adjust our mindset and decide that this is what I'm going to do regardless of what happens. I'm going to do what He has always intended for me because I was born for this and nobody else can do it like I can. Nobody else can do what I've been inaugurated to do. Although there are other people that have the same kind of gifts and callings, nobody can do it like me.

Every one of us is unique in our own way. God made us unique. Uniqueness is a powerful thing that God has created in humanity so that we won't confuse our unique purposes on this earth with others. Uniqueness is amazing. Just think about it. He didn't make us clones. He gave us all distinct features, a DNA profile, finger prints, and more that is *inimitable* to only you—As it is in the natural, so it is in the spirit. So accept who you are. Nobody else is like you. People may try to imitate and emulate you, but nobody is just like you. Nobody can be you but you. We may share some genes and traits from our spiritual parents (mentors), but you can't be an exact remake of them. You have to develop your own spiritual identity because you're the only one who can become who you are. God only created one you; one who is unique with a specific destiny and you are the only one who can fulfill it. Yet, God is sovereign and he will not allow the lives of those who are to be impacted by your obedience to suffer if you do not walk in your purpose. However, your purpose will suffer if you do not walk in your divine assignment.

As I previously stated, before God created the heavens and the earth I was in God's heart; his plan—and now—I AM learning to walk through the plan every day. I'm in the process of life and on the journey of becoming what I was in the heart of God. I pray you understand this fully. This book is about helping you discover and settle with the purpose you were predestined to manifest— to walk in total divine fulfillment.

The journey and process can be lonely at times. There are some good days and some bad days. There are some good times and some bad times. There are some negative influences and some positive influences. However, each one of those experiences, influences, and circumstances surrounding our lives are all a part of the journey that will help us to become great and successful in the eyes of God, not necessarily in the eyes of man.

Therefore, we have to take advantage of opportunities to feel and experience pain, to go through hurts, to go through rejection and every other kind of situation that we don't want to experience. They're actually good for you, although not seemingly good to you, **nevertheless,** there is a glory that will accompany that season of pain and trials. You'll never get the *exaltation* any other way. It will not come through your good times—only through your pain. It won't come through those times when you're experiencing great joy, this *magnificence* will come when you're experiencing great sorrow and sadness—the times your fear is at its peak—and you are yet seeking, asking, longing and thirsting after God with your whole heart. No, the pain itself does not release the glory. It releases as you draw closer to the Father in the midst of it, without retreat.

I believe that one of the keys to overcoming on this journey is the belief in predestination. I truly believe according to the Scriptures that before the foundation of the world we were in the Father's heart. We were predestined in God to be a manifestation of His existence. When the processes and journey of life with all the pain and suffering; happiness and sadness; joy and sorrow all comes together, it brings us to a place called **destination.** This is necessary because we have to come to the place where we know God in the power of His resurrection and the fellowship of His suffering. Of course that's easier said than done when you're walking through a trial—it's the time when you confront your will to choose. You must make a decision that you're going to accomplish the assignment by walking fully through the difficulty trusting God.

There has to be a confrontation between your will, which is your power of choice (your power to choose and decide), and that which you fear. You could decide to confront it or turn back and digress from what could be the greatest season of your life or learn how to face and overcome those fears that have held you hostage.

I also believe your seasons of pain, struggle, sorrow, and suffering are the greatest opportunities for thanksgiving. Thanksgiving and gratitude are two of the greatest tools that we can utilize during times of pain and uncertainty. When we give God thanks, we identify Him in the midst of our situation. We acknowledge that he is present with us. It's like praying to the Father and saying, *"I love you through all of this, I trust you with all of this, and I know that you are with me. I am going to patiently wait for You to bring the change. And Lord, please allow me to receive what I need to receive and to get the treasure out of this season of time."*

God loves to be shown love. And He loves to be thanked and acknowledged by His creation. The Bible tells us to trust in the Lord with all our hearts and not to lean on our own understanding, but to acknowledge him in all our ways and he'll direct our path. When we appreciate God, we open God's heart to us. He wants to direct us and extend his favor, but there are prerequisites for obtaining and unlocking God's promises in our lives. It's not God's will for us to suffer, but it is certainly an opportunity for God to show His best hand. If we want Him to be blessed by us, we must exalt and appreciate Him while we're going through. Your perseverance delights God's heart.

Everyone, especially Believers, needs to learn the value of suffering because it's a part of life. You can't live in this earthly realm and not go through difficulty. There's simply no escaping it; it is impossible, so, don't live in a fantasy world. Wake up! If anyone thinks they're never supposed to go through anything or suffer any loss, then they're in denial. "Ecclesiastes 3" tells us that there is a "time and season for everything under heaven"; yet, we know God will never put more on us than we can bear. If we are dealing with "IT", then we can go through it.

This book is based on several of my sermons on seasons of struggle that illustrate the process of life that God is taking us through. I believe the lessons shared in this book are important in gaining an understanding of the purpose of the Kingdom of God in the earth.

- First, we will examine the life of Joseph. Joseph was a dreamer and a move of God always starts with a dream.

- Second, we will study the relationship between Elijah the prophet and his protégé Elisha. It is fitting here to portray the process of life through what I'll characterize as the "Prayer Journey." No matter where we are in the journey of life, prayer should always be our posture.

- Third, we will take a closer look at the "Prayer Journey." In it are what I will call the four levels of prayer—Gilgal, Bethel, Jericho and Jordan—followed by the Kingdom Advancement where the development of the corporate body is discussed in measure.

- Fifth and finally, we will look at the Fifth Dimension—where prevailing and crossing over Jordan propels us to the place you were predestined. The place where you step over into your Destiny!

Are you ready to take your journey? It is imperative to stay focused and alert so that you don't lose momentum in the most pivotal hour… the grand ascent. Just like Queen Esther, you're destined for the throne to bring deliverance to many.

REFLECTION AND STUDY QUESTIONS

1. One of the keys to overcoming on this journey is the belief in predestination. How does predestination impact our complete and total lives?

2. Define the word "destiny." What does this word mean to you?

3. What are your unique abilities in what God has endowed you with? How are you using those abilities to *influence* the world around you?

4. Coming full circle is a journey about becoming who God has predestined you to be in Him. What do you believe you are predestined for?

5. Has there been a confrontation with your will vs. the will of God? If so, describe this struggle.

SECTION II

GOD STARTS WITH

A DREAMER

A Planted Seed

The dream all began with a seed planted by the Creator, our Father in heaven. God knows exactly what that seed is going to grow and become—the present and the future. God has already deposited all of the necessary ingredients into the seed for it to grow and mature to its purpose. You might ask how do we know that we are going to become what has been prophesied over us? How do we know that we will have what we say? Alternatively, how do we know that what we believe we will one day come into existence?

How does a farmer know that he will get corn when he plants seeds? He knows because the manufacturer the 'Author of Life' has already pre-dispensed what is in that seed and what it will become. So the farmer has faith based on what he has learned in life that this particular seed when planted will one-day manifest corn. His faith doesn't look to get peas; nor will he get peas because he's confident that he planted corn seed. He goes through the process of planting, nurturing and cultivating until the time of harvest. He's looking for corn and when he comes one day he's going to find it.

Likewise, God plants seeds into our hearts through dreams, visions, spoken prophetic words and the written Word. But we are made in God's image and we have power. We have free will and choice. We can reject the seed by rejecting the word. However, if we take that word and nurture it in our hearts, then we can grow into what God has predestined us to become.

Just as it is classified in science, there are numerous kingdoms. You have the Plant kingdom and the Animal kingdom. People are like God. We can create and build, but we can also destroy. Because of our ability to choose to create or destroy, it's more difficult to see the process and determine from the outset what our destiny will be; therefore, we must look to the manufacturer of the product . . . The destiny is sealed by God. The process can be prolonged because of wrong choices that causes delays.

A COAT OF MANY COLORS

When I was growing up, God the Father planted seeds into my heart. I always thought of myself as a type of Joseph. I felt that I had a coat of many colors. I grew up in a family where there were nine of us. I always thought that I was very unusual; unique in my own way so I kind of felt like a Joseph. Although, there were many odd moments however, I knew my life was special because of the several abilities the Holy Spirit endowed me. I had favor and could get things done. This blessedness was part of God's treasure to be shared and imparted to the next chosen one to carry the mantle.

Just as God gave Joseph a dream, I too had a great dream; in order for the realization of that dream to manifest I had to walk out the process just as Joseph was intimately acquainted with the struggle of obeying, and believing God to fulfill his purpose. Joseph's dream was unique in that his dream appeared to be larger than life to those around him. He was destined for greatness, but being a child could not comprehend the enormity of what God had planned for his life; he simply did not understand it. So the Bible tells us in Genesis 37 that Joseph had a dream and when he told it to his brothers, they hated him and then he had a second dream:

> *"And he dreamed yet another dream, and told it to his brothers, and said, 'Behold, I have dreamed a dream more; and, behold, the sun and the moon and the eleven stars made obeisance to me.' And he told it to his father, and to his brethren: and his father rebuked him, and said unto him, what is this dream that thou hast dreamed? Shall thy mother, thy brethren, and I, indeed come to bow down ourselves to thee to the earth? And his brethren envied him; but his father observed the saying."* (Genesis 37: 9-11)

So here, we see that God plants a seed of divine purpose in Joseph's heart by way of two separate dreams emphasizing double impact. Perseverance on the journey is always vital, and some of you are going to receive double for your trouble. Joseph is just a young boy and unskilled in divine communications, thus becomes a target of the enemy to derail and had many attempts assailed to physically destroy him.

He may have seemed like he was bragging to them. He may have seemed cocky and arrogant, but he was just a young boy. So when he had the second dream that confirmed the first one his brothers hated him even more and his father rebuked him.

His father was his spiritual covering. This is a lesson for parents, the story exemplifies that there are times when God may reveal to your children information to influence the entire family or even a nation, and may not necessarily reveal his entire plan to the parents at that time. Why? Because God said, "out of the mouth of babes will come wisdom." (ref. Mat. 11:25) He also said, "He chooses the foolish things, the weak things of the world to confound the wise." So "no flesh will glory in His presence." (ref. 1 Cor. 27, 29)

This process reveals why we must become as little children in order to enter into the kingdom of God (ref. Mat. 18:3). Parents, your children feel safe knowing they have you as the protector, provider and comforter… they don't have a care in the world.

As parents, it is easy at times to not listen to your children because they are children, however, as fathers and mothers it's important that we have an ear to hear our children. Not everything that comes out of their mouths is foolishness. They might not get it all right and say it using the "spiritual jargon" that we have become accustomed to hearing, but as you listen, you will know that God is using them, and he speaks through them too. It may just be a test to see if you will hear God when a *donkey* speaks. Balaam was tested like this and failed. (Refer to Num. 23)

Jacob's favoritism of Joseph created tremendous jealousy towards him from his brothers to the point where they hated him. Jacob certainly didn't mean his son any harm for loving him like he did, but his love sets Joseph up to be despised and hated by his brothers. Hence, they desired to kill him. To the brothers, their father's love for Joseph was toxic. *This is also a lesson for parents that we have to love all of our children the same. Of course, it's human nature to connect with one child more than another, which may appear to be favoritism, but your love should never play favorites. Sibling rivalry spawns jealousy, which can be dangerous, fatal, like a ticking time bomb.* In this case, Joseph was propelled into an abyss of what seemed like an endless pit of pain, tribulation, and sorrow as a result of the jealousy of his brothers.

Joseph went through thirteen years of hell! He lost complete control over his life, but God was in control, even if it didn't look that way. If he were going to get out of this one, then God would have to do it. Yet, after all those years and everything he went through Joseph still carried the promise—destiny. His brothers' concern was that Joseph might one day rule over them didn't matter. It is man's order that ascribe to the first-born the blessing of the father. However, that wasn't God's plan. Sometimes God will disappoint man's order to get His plan done.

God will not be placed in a box; yet, everything he does is holy—it is right and it is true and it will line up with His words. The Bible says 'there's nothing new under the sun.' So just because God does not act according to your plan, does not mean you can come up with your own theology or write your own Bible. It's still holiness or hell, right or wrong, blessings or curses, life or death.

The Bible even says that they hated Joseph for the words he spoke to them. That's powerful! It is proof that words are more than just words. They carry power. They are active. The word of God *is* power! It's active. It is alive. Even as you read this prophetic word, in your belly (or soul), a movement is happening; the word of God is making room for you to give birth to a dream that will create room for you.

Finally, God set up the circumstances with the king of Egypt that would lead to Joseph being brought out of the pit, right to the throne. So don't limit yourself. You are destined for the throne. Joseph symbolized Christ. In addition, when we become born again, our new nature must represent a type of Christ; we must become the expressed image of Christ

Jesus in the earth… although we are spiritually seated with him in heavenly places. (Ref. Ephesians 2:6)

Eventually, Joseph's dreams came to pass when he was appointed the second ruler in Egypt by the king. God used him to save his entire family, including his brothers who hated him, from a famine that came into the land. Because Joseph had a kingdom assignment, his dreams were larger than life (or so it appeared).

WALK OUT YOUR DREAM

The process of life is all about walking out that dream and becoming what you were predestined to become. You may be saying, Joseph went through thirteen years of hell but mine feels like its twenty years of hell. I forewarn you that in your trial, you can become so battle fatigued and weary, and weariness is extreme physical tiredness. You will deal with emotional weariness or even spiritual weariness, especially when you're in transition and making progressive movement.

For example, when you're traveling a long distance in a car, the movement of riding can take a toll on your body even if you're not driving. If you're going a long distance, you can get worn out by just riding in a vehicle. The scripture says, *be not weary in well doing for you shall reap in due season if you faint not*. So don't be weary. You're about to come into a due season where you will reap. God is going to increase your strength. But weariness comes to stop you from moving forward so don't pay attention to it. God will give you wisdom.

Don't be foolish. You have to know when to go and when to be still, because many times in the church we tend to believe that you are just supposed to go, go, and go all the time. If you're constantly going, when do you have time to hear God? Some weariness is self-imposed. That's why wisdom is so essential. A lot of damage can be caused by a lack of wisdom because it doesn't matter what you know; it matters how and when you use what you know.

LIVE IN THE SPIRIT REALM

While we're in a move of God and have momentum, we need to learn how to be still. We need to stop doing some of this running and unnecessary movement. Sometimes we're moving around so much when we need to just be still and get into God's presence. "They that wait on the Lord's presence shall renew their strength." There's a renewal that God wants you to experience as you wait on him.

We are doing too many unnecessary things. You cannot be all things to all people. Learn how to say no. In this season, you cannot have people making you run all over the place. Learn how to set boundaries and stick to them. It's important to minimize telephone time; to reduce the hours spent watching television and surfing the internet so you can maximize your time with the Father. You MUST learn to shut it all down and get into God's presence and hear Him!

Where are you right now? A lot of things are going on in the spirit, and God is moving on our behalf. But, just because God is moving, do not think that Satan is not at work too. Some of the weariness that you're feeling is a result of the enemy at work. That's why it's important to stay in the Lord's presence so that you'll be able to discern the difference between a work of God and that of the adversary. You want to know if the tiredness you're experiencing is a physical tiredness and you need to rest, or if it's an attack of the devil. If it's a spiritual attack, you want to know how to deal with the *"type"* of spirit that's coming against you. God is trying to show us how to live in the spirit; to follow his leading and learn to recognize the activity in the spirit realm more clearly.

When you live submissively in the spirit, you are sensitive, alert and aware; the spirit of God gives you discernment to let you know what it is that you're facing in life. It's important not to get confused by your emotions. It's much deeper. It's tapping into an awareness that can only be seen and sensed by the enlightenment of the Holy Spirit. Not that you won't feel anything. You may even question. *What am I feeling? What is this? Wait a minute!* You're not letting things just fly over your head. You become aware and stop being insensitive. You realize that the devil isn't just flying over your head, but he's building a nest. Stop living as if you're immune to the attacks and antics of the enemy. He's out to destroy your influence, and ultimately your destiny.

And so there is a realm in the spirit that God wants us to live in all the time. People of God, we've got to go to the next dimension in God. You must live out of the realm of the spirit where you do not entertain the lust and *impulses* of the flesh. Having this depth of awareness enlightens you; the Spirit of God will reveal what demonic activity is in operation and how you are to deal with it. Don't ever under-estimate this—it's imperative to know when you're dealing with the devil. If you don't know, you had better know. Wake up! It's time to be aware of the devil's traps and snares. The devil is coming to you as an angel of light and too many of us are being tricked! Don't be fooled!

COMMAND YOUR SOUL!

God wants you to get still. Be still and be patient. Wait for the Lord! Wait in His presence because God has a word. He wants to speak to you. We need a word from the Lord! We all need God to speak to us. But it's vital to get still in your spirit. Now, you can be physically still, yet your spirit is still going. What I mean is when your soul man is still raging, you have to command it to be quiet and still. The Bible says waiting on the Lord requires quietness in your soul.

Say this prayer:

I speak to my soul and command my soul to be quiet in the name of Jesus. Be still my soul! God is going to see me through. I will not be anxious for anything. I will not fret nor be afraid. God has not given me a spirit of fear and he will never put more on me than I can bear. I do not have a care, because I'm casting my cares on God. I am more than a conqueror. I am an overcomer. I will not yield. I will not go under. I command my peace to be still in Jesus' name I pray. Amen.

The devil wants you to have an anxiety attack. He wants you to go under. He wants you to have a breakdown. But, you have to decree and declare that *I will not have a breakdown, I'm having a breakthrough! I'm breaking through the enemy's camp! I'm breaking through this battle!* It's time to move again. God's growing you up fast. You don't have time to set up camp and entertain the enemy. You can't stay where you were last week. Arise! It is not the rest God has ordained. Do not stay in a place after God's presence has left. There is no more grace, and it will cause death. The place is defiled and it will cause utter destruction.

In this process, we're coming full circle to our purpose, which is the fulfillment that God is trying to bring us to complete culmination. This thing, as they say it is *"coming to a head."* Akin to when you have a big blister on your hand or foot, a blister can result from friction against the skin, burning, freezing, chemical exposure, or infection. It can start out as something seemingly harmless; like a little bump, but after a while, it starts getting sore and begins to fill with pus. After a fluid-filled pocket forms, to bring it to a head pressure has to be applied. It may even be necessary to take something sharp to pierce it in order to release the fluid (which is infected). And that's what has been happening in the spirit. God's trying to bring things to a head. He's trying to cause the ministry in your belly to flow out of your hurt and pain to bring healing to you and to others that you're destined to impact.

THE OIL OF THE ANOINTING

The reason for some of the weariness you're feeling is because God desires to stretch out in you. When God pours into your spirit, you must pour out of yours. You do not want the oil of the anointing to cease in your life. Don't let a week go by that you don't pour out somewhere to somebody in some situation. And the only way you're going to stay fresh and have room to receive fresh oil is that you must empty out. God wants you to have fresh oil on a daily basis. You cannot release a fresh anointing, or have a fresh ministry out of your belly on a daily basis if you don't pour out daily. You've got to pour out somewhere, even if it's just a smile. If it's just a hello, just a hug, just telling somebody Jesus loves you. If somebody comes and says that they are sick, well say let's pray. God wants you to become a drink offering pouring yourself out that others may be able to drink from the fresh oil and fresh water that's in you. However, wisdom is always principle. In Matthew7:6, the Bible advises us not to throw our pearl to pigs, because they will trample them and destroy you. You've got to discern the body and know whom the

Father is leading you to pour into. Everyone is not ready or able to receive what is in you.

However, you have to pour out to chosen groups and or individuals in order to get more. If you don't pour out, you'll become stagnate in God. You'll go right back to your old form that will be worse. That comfortable, old dead place of just maintenance won't be the same; you will plummet further into spiritual darkness if you don't allow God to redirect your steps. God doesn't want to just maintain your life; He wants you to go from glory to glory. There's a progression in God. There's increase, movement, and momentum. God is ongoing; He is progressive. To Him there is no end!

We can't live without the oil of the anointing. Without it, we begin to experience sterilization and barrenness, where *spiritual* pregnancy cannot take place; ultimately leading to *spiritual* death. We cannot survive without the anointing of the Holy Spirit present in our lives and in the church. No birthing can take place from a dead body. Once the body dies, the life that was once growing inside to be birthed out one day, dies with it.

FOCUS ON FAITH IN THE WILDERNESS

We must press through with our faith! The press helps fight past the weariness that will cause us to stand still if we don't push. That's what would happen to the children of Israel every time they came to a hard place. Whenever they would become weary, they would start mumbling and complaining. Weariness leads to disobedience and rebellion. They could not be satisfied. Everything was a burden and whatever God told Moses to do just wasn't right in their eyes. Because they were tired from traveling, they began to focus on their flesh. Spiritual weariness is not just something that happened back then, we still contend with it today, often with the same response as the children of Israel. However, we know God doesn't hear or respond to our murmuring and complaining.

Moses said to the children of Israel, we've got to go by the way of the Red Sea; but, they looked back and they saw the enemy. Immediately, they began to complain and they were just getting started. Let me say this, we are just getting started in what God wants to do. We can't think that we have made it yet. This new day is just getting started. We're just coming into what God has ordained for this last hour. The church is just now tapping in to what God has ordained for the church for this hour to accomplish the will of God. So we're just getting started. Don't get caught up.

So when they saw the enemy—oh God! Then they said to Moses, "You brought us out of Egypt, from a place where we were in bondage, but at least we had garlic and food to eat. Let us alone! We rather serve the Egyptians. We should've stayed in bondage. You should've left us alone while it was going good. We were comfortable in our bondage.

You should've left us there. You brought us out and now you're going to let us die out here in the wilderness! What's the difference?"

Die on your way to victory as opposed to being out of the will of God and dying out of the will of God? You will not die on your way to victory! (I can't prevent some hardship, however, I'm going to die on my way to the Promise Land. I'm going to die trying.) So the children of Israel shut they're mouth.

They opened their mouths, and they became weary. Weariness is not just a physical thing. It is also demonic—a demonic devil that came from fear. When you get under a tormenting spirit of fear, there's fatigue, depression, heaviness and tiredness that accompanies that spirit. You'll become so tired you can't lift one foot up. You can hardly climb stairs and you think that you are sick; but, it's nothing but a demonic weariness. Why? It's because they complained and murmured against God. That's why it's important that you don't open your mouth against God's purpose.

If you open your mouth, say something good. Say something about the word. Prophesy! Prophesy over your purpose! Prophesy to the devil about your purpose! Tell every enemy you encounter, "I'm going to the nations," if that's what God says. Prophesy your assignment. Tell that devil, "You can't depress me, depression! Fear you are a lie! You can't stop me because God told me I'm going to the nations! "He said I will preach among thousands." What did God say to you? Speak it! Prophesy!

Do not merely speak about your problem, but speak the solution, which is your prophetic word to set change in motion. Use the WORD. My word says… You might think prophecy isn't imperative, but it is extremely important. You take that prophecy and beat the devil back with it. Take your prophecy and whip his head. War with your prophecy! War with it! That's your weapon. 3

YOUR DREAM WILL BRING YOU OUT

Remember Joseph, that's what he did. The scriptures say when Joseph's word came—his chains fell off! Thirteen years of hell! However, when his word came, he remembered that dream. He remembered that prophetic dream. You got to be a dreamer. Don't let the devil steal your dream. He remembered the dream! His brothers threw him in the pit because of the dream. It was because of the prophecy he was thrown into the pit to be killed! But the prophecy, his dream, that exact word spoken over his life brought him out of the pit! It caused a divine connection to show up, bring him out, and take him where God positioned him. Where God wanted him for that dream to come to pass thirteen years later.

So you got to tell the devil: I'm a dreamer. I have a dream. Do you remember your dream? Tell God to bring that dream back whether it was an open eye dream or closed eye, it was prophetic for you; and, that dream is going to bring you out of the hell you're in. I don't care how long you've been there. I don't care how tough it's getting. That dream that's in your belly and the word of the Lord that's been spoken to you ten years ago is going to bring you out, to bring you in so you can fulfill your assignment. There's a designated people, a designated place, a designated anointing, a designated mandate, for a designated assignment for you.

So wait on the Lord! Wait for him! Surely, it shall come to pass. You got to tell yourself: My dream is not over. It's just in the beginning. I'm going to birth what God has impregnated me with. I shall overcome! I have a dream. I don't care what nobody says. Where you are now is not where you will be. God's going to shock you out of your boots. Watch God!

God told me in my office, he said, "I'm getting ready to do something quick! That's why you can't put your hand on nothing. You can't get a fix on nothing! You can't set up camp no-where. You can't just get satisfied because I'm moving so fast." So wait on the Lord. He said, "I took you out five years ago and I brought you back to take you in. I took you out to take you in! Now you're about to fulfill your destiny. The dream that I gave you and your husband twenty-five years ago for this ministry is about to come to pass." That is why God began positioning the right people in the house for an assignment.

When God positions you, you're designated. God ordained! Handpicked and I encourage you to hold on to your dream. Your assignment is huge! The bigger your battle the bigger the blessing! Some of you got thirty; some sixty, and some are walking up under a one-hundred-fold blessing.

The prophetic word came forth out of my spirit that there was an impartation that had to happen through writing, and here it is four years later. Yes, God starts with a dreamer and the end of a thing spoken is just the beginning. There is a process and that process consists of a journey of prayer.

REFLECTION AND STUDY QUESTIONS

1. Has God deposited a dream seed in to you by way of a dream, the spoken prophetic word or his written word? What is that dream?

2. What is the process by which your promise will happen?

3. Have you fully surrendered and allowed God to have full control of your life, the process and the outcome like Joseph?

4. Have you overcome weariness and battle fatigue? How must you stay in this place of victory?

5. Are you allowing God to pour fresh oil into your spirit man daily? And are you pouring out daily to someone in need?

6. Are you walking as a living stone in your home; the marketplace, the church or wherever your footsteps tread?

7. In your walk with God, are you focusing on faith or are you focusing on fear? In what ways are you demonstrating your focus?

SECTION III

THE PRAYER JOURNEY:

"DO ME AGAIN JESUS"

JOURNEY OF A BELIEVER

In that place called process, we are all being developed for God's purposes and being formed into the image of Christ Jesus. You can't find a great man or a great woman of God unless they spend much time with God in consecration and prayer. You can tell when an individual or a church has been in a season of consecration because there is a weightiness of God's presence there. You don't have to do a whole lot of work. Neither do you have to do a whole lot of sweating when God's presence is there and whatever you desire or need, you can just pull it right out of the atmosphere. God's presence propels you into a "right now season"! You must believe that in order to receive it.

Normally my niche is that of a preacher, but God put me in a place of teaching in this season of my life. Teaching wasn't a place that I was comfortable with because I'm used to just preaching and hyping folks up, but in a place of teaching, it's a prerequisite to be still and release the word to people. I believe that the order of the last day ministry is teaching. I believe that God is calling leaders now to stretch beyond a lot of the hyping stuff that we've been experiencing; it's time now to settle down. There is a time that God will use us to exhort and to bless you with the hype and all of that, but I believe that this is a time that the people of God need to be taught the word. It is paramount for one's spiritual growth to be connected to a solid teaching ministry where the word of God is thoroughly taught.

Many people don't have that kind of ministry. It's all hype with no teaching. Therefore, the people never experience transformation. They never experience change. They never grow up and mature, and become all that God has ordained them to be. It's time to grow up. There is a *massive* release of power, and a greater work that God has ordained for the church to *"manage"* during this hour. God has even more for you than what you are even walking in now. He said, "Greater Things" so church we have not walked in the "GREATER THINGS" in its fullness, but I believe we're getting ready to walk in the greater things of God.

God is calling leaders to walk into expansive realms of anointing, miracles, and revelation, and as we begin to teach the people of God, we are going to see the great works coming out of the pews. God is going to use you that are in the pews. It's not just coming from the pulpit only. God is going to use you to lay hands on the sick, to cast out devils and to bring healing. I believe that you will walk by people and your shadow will heal them. This is that the hour; people are looking for miracles, so what are we waiting for? God is waiting for us. We're not waiting on

God. This is the hour that God wants to use us to walk in the greater things that he preordained for us to walk in.

The 2nd book of Kings, chapter two contains significant insights into walking in this level of power and demonstration of greater works. Even though I've taught on this passage of scriptures before, I have never taken it in this direction, which pertains to prayer. But I'm going to talk about a journey that Elijah and Elisha took just as Elijah was getting prepared to take his flight to heaven.

Elijah was at the end of his life, and he was on his way out. He had fulfilled his purpose and his destiny. He had mentored this young man (Elisha) who had walked with him and served him for many years. At this particular time, Elijah is getting ready to take his flight. Before he leaves this earth, he is going to take this young man on a final journey with him and it is a journey of prayer. In this process that accompanies this journey, Elisha had set his heart to follow the man of God. Subsequently, the Bible says:

"When the Lord was about to take Elijah up to heaven by a whirlwind, Elijah and Elisha were traveling from Gilgal. And Elijah said to Elisha, "Tarry here, I pray you (or request of you), for the Lord has sent me to Bethel." But Elisha replied, "As the Lord lives and as your soul lives, I will not leave you." Therefore, they went down to Bethel. (cf. 2 Kings, 2, AV)

In this passage of scripture, they are on a four-part journey that I've termed the Four-levels of prayer or the Prayer journey. I'm going to take you through this four-part journey—as God revealed to me as the Four-levels of a journey of prayer:

FIRST LEVEL OF PRAYER: GILGAL

The first place Elijah and Elisha were positioned at during the time of their transition was Gilgal. On this journey, they departed from Gilgal en route to Bethel. Gilgal means a memorial site; it's between Jordan and Jericho where Israel practiced circumcision after the people had crossed over with the Ark. Here they set up a memorial at a place where they were grieving over their past failures and gloating over their past triumphs.

However, they must move on. Likewise, you must move on! So Gilgal represents a place on this journey of prayer where God is going to test our faithfulness. He's going to test our love. He's going to test your ability to remain consistent and endure to the place of process. And it begins first with relationships. Now Gilgal is a place called "Circle." It's a place of the circle—a place where faith is tested.

Gilgal is a place where faith is born out of pressure. If you're going to experience the *greater things* of God and to be used by God to do bigger works, you're going to have to experience pressure and learn how to endure in the process. You must be able to remain consistent and endure through the place of process and it begins first with relationship— a relationship with God.

Gilgal is a place of circumcision—the cutting away. What is God going to cut away in us? He's going to cut away carnal things! He said, "no flesh will glory in His sight." In other words, the glory of God is not going to rest on your flesh, your fleshly works. God wants every person alone to cut away his flesh (to put carnality under submission). The operative word here is "alone" to cut away your flesh. This is the hour now that God is going to pull you away from relationships, separate you from family members (not where there is a breach that is not what I'm talking about), but God is going to pull you away from that which is comfortable for you. He is going to pull you away from those things that have been your strength. He is going to pull you away from things that you have depended on. This is the hour that God is going to get you alone to Himself. He wants time with you.

MEMORIALIZING YOUR PAST

So Elijah and Elisha are on this journey and they are heading to a place called Bethel. But they must get out of Gilgal first. You got to get out of Gilgal. You got to come out of that place where you're memorializing your past and you're gloating over your triumphs. You got to come out of that place where you're memorializing your hurts, your rejections and everything that everybody has done to you, and your un-forgiveness. You have to come out of that place and move on to Bethel.

You're on a journey. God dictates that it will be a place where He wants to be alone with you — a place where He is trying to build faith in you. It is a place where there is pressure. God is saying this is the place where He is developing in you the tools that you will need for the next season of life. He says until you get through this you cannot move. Many of us are in this place, and we haven't moved yet because we're still memorializing our pain. We're still dealing with those past tests that we've been through.

We're in a cycle. God wants to break that cycle and eradicate the mental bondage that you are carrying year-after-year. I am talking about that place where you go through the same old thing every year, same time every year, same pain, same struggle every year! God says you got to come out of there! Come on out! You got to come out of Gilgal to get to Bethel. That's where your cycles are broken.

So as they are journeying—right here is where Elijah says to him "you don't have to go with me." But Elisha says, "as the Lord liveth as your soul liveth, I will not leave thee." This is the place where you got to get in your mind and say, I'm not coming out until I get my breakthrough. I'm going to get fully delivered! That's why there are so many problems and struggles in the church because people are not getting fully delivered. You can't come to a place of completeness if you keep cycling in old behaviors and life patterns.

So Elijah and Elisha are coming out of Gilgal, they are now heading to a place called Bethel. The Bible says and they go down to Bethel: (for further study on Bethel see Genesis 28)

SECOND LEVEL OF PRAYER: BETHEL

Now here Bethel means a place of testing. It's not over yet! Sometimes we think Oh, I'm so anointed! I've made it through. I finally got my breakthrough. I just broke through my cycles and I just got over my past, but it's not over yet. You still got to go to Bethel; and, here Bethel is a place of testing, trials and tribulations—a place where ministry is built up.

PREORDAINED FAMILY DYNAMICS

Part of the process of testing involves the removal of memorials and putting the past behind. You need to know who you are and to know your family dynamics. You must get a firm grip on your past, deal with it internally and accept that it was what it was—a part of the test. You were foreordained to be born into the family that you were born in and so was I.

We have to deal with our **Identity Complex**. As I was growing up, I kind of resented growing up in a home that was poor. I've to share this testimony many times, and here it's needful again because some of you reading this book are identifying with this. Perhaps you are identifying with this because you resent having been raised in a large family. Or you resent being raised in a family where you didn't really feel a part of it. Or perhaps for some other reasons you felt that your family was dysfunctional which in a sense everybody's family is dysfunctional.

Perhaps you think that you were ill favored because you were raised in a certain family; whether it was poor, whether your father was a drug addict, or your mother was an alcoholic or that your father was born on the streets. Let me tell you it doesn't matter what family you were born in even if your father was the President of the United States. It doesn't matter to whom you were born; it was meant to be and you need to understand that. You need to get a hold of that and get the value out of that.

There's a *treasure* even in your family dynamics. Different conditions and circumstances in life, perhaps caused your parents to go in unreliable ways as far as the way they lived, and the choices they made which had nothing to do with you. But it had to do with their life situation and circumstances with their own particular mindsets and beliefs. So you may have resented having grown up in your family as I did, which I did because it was poor—dirt poor; but our precious mother always gave us her very best. I have much appreciation and love in my heart for the memories of her and for the things that she did as a mother. She loved us with such tremendous, undying love. Her love was awesome and that's the way I love my children. Yet our home was poor, and I resented it. I had a love/hate relationship for my father. Still I was ordained to be born into that family.

In all of that, I always had something special in me. I always felt greatness inside of me. I always felt success in me. I always felt that it was more to me than what I was growing up to live like. My mother taught us etiquette. She taught us wonderful things. I said that to say this: It doesn't matter how you were born or to whom you were born; it doesn't matter who your mother or father were or whatever family you were born in. You may love your family deeply or you may have a love/hate feeling for them. You may resent them or you may wish you had never been born to that family. It doesn't matter because you have greatness on the inside of you. You need only to look to God and look within.

So Elijah and Elisha come to Bethel—the second level, that place of testing, tribulations—a place of process even from family hang-ups. Likewise, you got to go through Bethel. You can't just hang out there either. You can't set up a tent. You got to go through your place of testing. You have to hang in there. You got to go through your trials and tribulations. You have to go through that place of process; that place where ministry is being developed in order to enter the next level successfully.

THIRD LEVEL OF PRAYER: JERICHO

Elijah and Elisha are proceeding on their journey. They're now headed to a place called Jericho and the fourth verse reads, Elijah said to him, "Elisha, tarry here, I pray you, for the Lord has sent me to Jericho." But he said, "As the Lord lives and as your soul lives, I will not leave you." So, they came to Jericho. (cf. 2nd Kings 2:4)

Satan's place—the place of war! This is the place where you learn warfare. This is the place where you have a confrontation with the devil himself. This is the place where you battle for your life. This is the place where you battle for your sanity. This is the place where you battle for your soul. It's called Jericho, a place of war—Satan's place.

As in the book of Joshua, Jericho is where Joshua fought a huge battle and the walls of that city came tumbling down. This is a place where you have to break through the walls that have hindered you from moving forward. I'm talking about those walls that have hindered you from reaching your potential. Many of you are sitting on potential because you have walls up. The enemy has put walls up around you and until you break through those walls, you will never fulfill your purpose.

Jericho is the place where you war for your life. You war for your future. You war for your Destiny. You war for the Prophetic words and the assignment that has been placed in you. You war for that dream. It is a place of a curse and place of devastation. Yet it is a place of training and preparation.

WHERE ARE YOU?

Either you are still in Gilgal, cycling, or you're in Bethel learning how to go through trials and tribulations (whether they are intrinsic or extrinsic) or a combination of both. Perhaps you're in Jericho were you're at war with Satan. Where are you?

This is a pertinent place—if you don't come out of Jericho it's over! If you don't defeat the enemy of your mind, if you don't defeat the enemy of your soul, if you don't defeat Satan in that place you will never reach your potential. That is the place where you live or die, sink or swim. Anybody that you see in the ministry on the front line are those who overcame the enemy and have overcome death. They overcame the battles in their mind. They conquered that place where Satan tries to literally take your mind from you. Only you can make the choice to either succumb to the enemy or defeat his tactics, but know this, once you overcome it, he can't come that way again.

So if you're still going through it, you're not out yet. That's the place where death comes and stand up in your face and you got to make a decision whether you're going to live or die. This is where you overcome cancer! This is where you overcome mental breakdown. This is where you overcome rejection. This is where you overcome abuse, the past of abuse. Where are you?

Wherever you are in this process, declare that you are coming out. Declare that you are not staying in this process. Say I'm coming out. But you got to go through it, not around it. You can't default. You can't abort it! You got to go through it with boldness and tenacity proclaiming: life hold on—death turn loose! Many times, you may feel like you just want to turn everything loose and just give up. But this is the place where you make up your mind, no matter what I have to go through, no matter what it costs to walk in the anointing that God is releasing in this hour, I'm going to make it. The price is high and it's going to cost you something.

EMPOWERED TO SUBDUE PRINCIPALITIES

Here you fight for your Prophetic Word. That's why prophecy is so vital. That's why Satan hates prophetic churches. That's why prophetic churches have the worst battles and go through the greatest struggles. Apostolic, Prophetic churches live under such accusation and slander—the embodiment of Satan where people sit in the church and slander with accusation—the Accuser of the Brethren spirit—it is the embodiment of Satan. They come to find fault. They come to inflict destruction and havoc in the church. These demonic forces attempt to keep those churches from moving forward, because those churches are empowered to take territories!

You are empowered to bring down principalities and powers and Satan knows it. You're empowered to bring Jezebel down. You're empowered to bring Absalom down (all those spirits that are disloyal) that sit up in the house of God and are disloyal to spiritual authority. God's getting ready to roar! Everything that's sitting up in the house of God that's not under spiritual authority, that's not seeking God, that's not walking in loyalty and faithfulness to God—the Holy Spirit of God is going to roar upon you! And when He roars, you're going to see folk going out of the church feet first. That was said under the unction of the Holy Ghost because it's a very pertinent time in the spirit right now. So everything that's out of order got to get in order.

So the battle ensued here in Jericho. This place is where the war is intensified and you're fighting for your life. You're fighting for your future. You're fighting for your Destiny. You're fighting for your family. You're fighting for everything that belongs to you that God says is yours. You're fighting for the promise. You're fighting for your prophecy. You're fighting for the dream. Here is the place where you make a decision to continue the journey. This is the place where there's no-one (nobody) to help you. This is a fight between you and the devil—a fight of faith. This is the battle that will determine whether you will make it or not.

The story reveals that at this stage the children of Israel were progressive. It represents that you cannot pitch a tent in your spiritual Jericho either. You cannot pitch a tent in your battle you have to keep moving. You have to continue to be progressive. You have to progress and proceed with all due diligence. This place represents severe testing, and it will determine whether you will fail God or you will please God and bless God, and this is when you'll start to receive your reward for being faithful to God in the battle.

SPIRIT OF DISTRACTION

So as they were proceeding, moving forward with God, Elijah said to him, "Tarry here, I pray you, for the Lord has sent me to Jericho." In addition, the fifth verse says, "The sons of the prophets who were at Jericho came to Elisha and said, 'Do you know that the Lord will take your master away from you today?' And he answered, "Yes, I know it; hold your peace."

The sons of the prophets came to him and said to him, "do you not know" … Now look who is here at Jericho: the hecklers, those negative voices, those Sanballats and Tobiahs that don't won't you to grow and be fruitful, that don't want you to make it, that don't want you to prosper. Those are the places where you will hear accusation and slander. This is where family members turn against you because they don't understand.

The sons of the prophets are at Jericho, waiting to confront Elisha. "Do you not know that today the Lord is going to take your master away?" they asked with the intention to distract him. In addition, he answered and said, "Yes I know it! Hold your peace."

He told them to just shut up. This is where you got to get *bolder* in the Lord. You have to get bold because you cannot allow others to disrupt your journey. You're on a course; you're on an expedition to get where God wants you. In this place, you have to silence the voice of the enemy that speaks to you. You have to silence those outside voices that speak to you attempting to distract you. They wanted Elisha to change his mind and change his attitude, so he would go another way. You got to keep your attitude right when circumstances are not conducive. Know that the enemy always comes to get you to go in another direction to do something different.

It's not over yet. No matter how far you've come, you were just processing to the real battle. You'll begin to understand the heartbeat of God and the rhythm of God in the new place. Therefore, don't get distracted from advancing; don't get detoured. Elijah had already been there, but Elisha needed to go. Thus, he followed close behind with locked-in, locked-down, bulldog tenacity! Refusing to let go! The storm is hitting Elijah not Elisha because he is following behind him. The storm is hitting the head, not you. You got to follow Jesus!

The disciples had that sense when the storm of life got so heavy that seventy disciples walked away and went back. The remaining twelve stayed. They said to Jesus "You got the words of life." Job said, "You know the way I take and when I come out, I'll come out as pure gold." I've been tried in the fire and I'm out! Now God can trust me with the major assignments now.

THE GREATEST SEASON

God spoke something to me. I already knew it, but when He said it, it was a revelation to me. The Lord said, "Veter, in your weakest times—those areas where you are weakest, is where I'm strongest." Like I said, I knew this, but it was something I needed to hear. He said, "Those weak places in you are my strength. So just because you're in a weak season doesn't mean that God can't use you." That's the season that God can really use you because you're absolutely dependent upon him.

I don't care where you are right now. You may be feeling like you're insignificant and unimportant. You may feel like God can't use you. You may say I don't have any word in my mouth. I don't have an anointing. The heaven is dry. I can't hear God. I'm in the wilderness. I'm in a deep valley and I can't get out.

However, this is the place where God will use you. You are more effective in this place than you are on the mountaintop. When you think you're at your greatest peak—your greatest anointing, that is when you're not at your greatest place. God will let you do it yourself. But when you're in a weak season, the season where you don't feel so good about yourself and things aren't going so good, and you are in danger of having no direction is the season God can utilize to be your greatest.

You see, one thing we try to do is emulate other ministries and other ministers. Therefore, we compare ourselves to others and you never can really measure up. You end up always trying to measure up. In addition, when you try to measure up to other people and to other ministries, you will never be able to because you will never see yourself complete because that's not your anointing.

This is similar to David when he was preparing to encounter Goliath. David refused to wear Saul's armor because it did not fit him. It hadn't been tested.

There's an anointing that goes with the process. The hell you're in—the hell you're going through - will not work fully for me. What I'm dealing with can only help you but it's not your anointing. That's for me. But there is a struggle that you have in your personal life that is just designed for you and for the anointing that God wants to release in you for the masses.

So here, David is on this trajectory; he is getting ready to come out of Jericho and now he is being processed out of Jericho. They've gone through training and preparation and now they're headed to the next level. We're going to another level. So Elijah said to him, "Tarry here, I pray you, for the Lord has sent me to the Jordan."

FOURTH LEVEL OF PRAYER: JORDAN

Jordan is a place of death and separation. That's why it's pertinent that you spend time with God in prayer. The Apostle Paul said I die daily. You got to put this flesh under daily—death and separation from your flesh, from your carnal nature, from your desires; from your own opinions, from your own ideas; from every religious spirit and from every negative attitude concerning yourself.

After you experience death and separation, this is where God can now say, "I'm going to reward you. You can ask me for anything you want." Jordan is a place where you can ask God for anything you want! After you have journeyed from Gilgal to Bethel, to Jericho and pass through those seasons, those levels and now you're heading into Jordan, to cross the Jordan, He says now I'm going to reward you. What do you want? He said to Elisha what do you want? Ask me. Are you in that position, in that place that you can ask God for whatever you want now? In addition, Elisha said, "I want a double portion of your anointing." What did Elisha mean?

NOW IT'S YOUR TIME!

The Lord showed me that Elisha was really asking for a double portion of that prayer mantle. He told me the mantle, the cloak, the coat that Elijah had, was really a prayer mantle. The mantle was a coat of authority. The mantle was a coat of prayer. The mantle was a coat of the glory. The mantle represented the Presence of God—the covering of the Presence of God. Now Elijah says to him "ask me for what you want". So Elisha says, "I want a double portion."

If Elisha asked him for a double portion, why would Elijah give him his coat if the coat didn't have some kind of symbolic meaning? What if Elijah's coat wasn't significant symbolically? What then would be the purpose in giving Elisha his coat? Ministering on this message at the podium, I had my mother's cape with me. The cape was in a bag in the church office and while I was getting ready for the service, the Lord said to me, "Take that cape off the hanger. You are now ready to wear it."

THE MANTLE OF PRAYER

Let me give you some background information. My mother was a powerful woman of God. She would put that cape on and she was a woman that walked in prayer. She lived prayer, breathed prayer, and ate prayer. Her whole life was prayer, souls and evangelism. She was powerful! When she prayed for you, the devil had to go! When she prayed for you, sickness and death had to go! So, the Lord told me to take it off the hanger because you are ready for it now.

Elisha could not get Elijah's coat until he was ready for it—he too had to process the transformation and remain ready while waiting on the promise. There's somebody's anointing for you too. God said to me, put your mother's cape on and wear it now because you're ready for it. The cape is symbolic of my mother's anointing and when I put it on that same anointing that my mother walked in was released into my life.

There are people's lives that I will touch, and tap into and cause things to happen for them, as they will for me. I'm somebody's divine connection as someone is my divine connection. I'm somebody's Elijah and someone else is my Elisha. I've also been an Elisha and thank God, I've matured to Elijah. I'm now walking in someone else's double portion and that was Mother Lena Lucas and my mother, Mother Margaret Hill. I received those mantles of God from these two women, especially my mother's mantle.

I received a great mantle from my mother at the time that she left this world. Two days prior to her demise, I went to the hospital to see her. She kissed me and told me that she loved me. At that point, I knew that something had been released to me, and I knew that she was going home to be with the Lord. The following Sunday morning after we buried her, that mantle fell on me so heavily! I suddenly became what I was predestined to become! I began to walk in the beginning of what I was in the Father's heart from the foundation of the world instead of who I thought I was.

You may think what I just said is weird, but it's not weird. I'm speaking the oracles of God. God had told me that same anointing that your mother walked in, you shall walk in. Many of you got grandmothers, grandfathers, mothers, and fathers that walked in the power of God. It's time now for the process. It's time now for you to go through the process so you can walk in that same anointing.

My mother's cape was specially made for her many years ago. Prior to God telling me that it was time to wear it, I never washed it, never cleaned it or anything. That mantle remained the same as when she wore the cape. It's similar to that of the Apostle Paul, when they took his clothes and cut them and made handkerchiefs, which he gave those pieces of cloths to the people that manifested miracles. As a result, people were healed and delivered. During a season for over nine months, we lay on the floor at our church in prayer on sheets. The Lord had told me to go buy these sheets and cover the altar. Therefore, I covered the floor with those sheets and we prayed over them for almost a year.

Then about four months later the Lord told me to cut them up and give every person at the conference a piece of that sheet. We got reports of the miracles of God that were happening: miracles of healing, people getting jobs. God changed and transformed families as a result of those prayer cloths. The prayer cloths did not possess any power. The prayer cloths were merely symbolic of the power and anointing that was released when we laid on those sheets day and night, shut in the church, fasting, praying, and seeking the face of God. God began doing wonders in our midst.

My sister had three tumors in her back on her spine. She had those tumors for ten years and she never told anyone. Finally, they got so bad that one of them started to ooze something out. The tumors were causing her to be paralyzed on her right side; her hand, leg, and her hip were in so much pain. The pain was so excruciating that she was popping pain pills. She didn't tell anyone what was going on, but one Sunday I laid hands on her back and all three of those tumors left. God totally healed her! We also experienced a husband and wife that were both deaf. The wife was deaf in both ears and God healed both of them. When she got healed, her husband who was standing right behind her was healed at the same time. There were eight people healed in their back at the same time that my sister got healed. God is doing some powerful things in the spirit.

This is the time that God wants us to release and manifest His power like never before in the body of Christ! That's why as an individual you've got to be processed; but there is also a corporate responsibility on this prayer journey. We are just as accountable for this corporate journey as we are for our personal spiritual life. You must take your individual walk along with the body of Christ fully in mind too. Before we conclude with the level of the Jordan, let us look at the processing of the church that co-exists simultaneously with your individual journey.

You must pass through those seasons from Gilgal to Bethel, to Jericho heading into Jordan, with the victory of the corporate body of Christ also in mind—where the individual and the church through this *process* is coming full circle to the image and the bride of Christ. It's at Jordan that God says, "I'm now going to reward you." The place of destiny where He can say: "Now it's your time!"

REFLECTION AND STUDY QUESTIONS

1.   Are you still in Gilgal cycling? Have you ever been in a place like Gilgal before? If so, describe the event where you found yourself cycling; going around that same mountain again like the children of Israel.

2.   Are you in a place of testing like in Bethel? Describe the circumstances surrounding your test.

3.   Have you had previous tests that are similar to your experience in Bethel? If yes, describe them and how you overcame.

4. Have you ever felt like you were in a place like Jericho fighting with Satan himself? If so, what happened? How did you handle it? And how did the spirit of God help you to handle it?

7. At Jordan, you take a death walk. Have you crossed over yet? Have you died to that carnal nature? Describe what's holding you back?

8. Do you spend adequate time with God in prayer? How can you prioritize your schedule for adequate prayer and Bible study time?

9. Identify family dynamics and weakness that tends to bind and limit you. You can recognize them as your greatest season if you acknowledge God in all your ways.

SECTION IV

APOSTOLIC KINGDOM ADVANCEMENT:

THE PROCESSING OF THE CHURCH
KEEPING IT REAL

As I said in this processing, we as individuals along with the church are coming full circle to the image and the bride of Christ. In order to complete the process and walk in victory we're going to have to get things right in the church. Let me say it again, if we are to walk in the manifested power of the Glory of God, we have to be transparent, accountable and get things right or God is going to strip us naked in front of everybody. We must stop perpetrating, be real and keep it real on this journey. We must take authority over every unclean spirit and everything that's not like God.

Rebuke those spirits! Rebuke the spirit of fear and intimidation in the name of Jesus! Renounce the spirit of passivity. Renounce the spirit of insecurity, for in your weakness, God's strength is made perfect. Weakness is where the anointing is. We got to speak over ourselves, speak over our situation: "Now God I decree in the name of Jesus that I'm walking into health, body, soul and spirit. In the name of Jesus, I decree myself free. I make a decision. I've decided to be free in the name of Jesus. Wash me, Lord!"

Satan will not stop the advancement of the church. He will not stop the advancement of the people of God no matter what device he uses.

One of his most diabolical devices is the tongue. The people of God need to learn to bridle their tongues. The same word that is spoken in your local church, you need to speak. You got to start conforming to the spirit of the house. God wants to do a fresh thing. He wants to do an overhaul. You know how those people on television are given a complete makeover; well God is going to do a makeover on us. So tell God: Do me again.

Some Christians have lost their fire and passion. You may not even know where you are going. You're struggling with what you're supposed to be doing. You have no direction. This is the time to say to God "do me again Lord." This is decision-making time: a time for greatness, a time for manifestation, a year of dominion, power and the supernatural. God is ready to do a mighty work with his corporate body, but he is requiring his people to come to another level of purification. So tell God to do you again.

Take control over whatever is hindering you. God has given you power over all the forces of the enemy: If it's a spirit of worry and anxiety, take control over it! Whatever's holding you back, take control over it and ask God to do you again; to wash you through and through;

to set you free so you can come forth as pure gold when you're tried in the fire. Then God can use you. He can completely use you when you're totally yielded. You may be in the fire right now and it feels like you're not going to come out. But God says I'm making you better. I am making you better than ever before . . . The choice is up to you now. I want to make you completely whole. In this trial, I am making you whole.

CORPORATE ASSIGNMENT

God is making you complete although it may not seem like it in this trial. God has done all that he's going to do as it pertains to getting us where he wants us and doing what he wants us to do. He has already done it. Now it's up to us. The work is already complete. It's finished! He has already done it. I don't know what the body of Christ is waiting for in this hour. We have already been given our assignments corporately. We already know that we're positioned for certain territories for.

So now, it requires us to make some wise decisions about what we're going to do as it pertains to our part in making things happen. You got to realize that you got a vital part in the ministry. You have a vital part to play to cause that ministry to become all that it's supposed to be. Push that thing. God has great plans for us and we have a very short time to do what it is God has called us to do. We don't have very much time left. Prophecy has been fulfilled already and right now Jesus could come at any moment.

Things are all lined up. Get in there and do what God has called you to do. What were you birthed in this earth to fulfill? What is your purpose in the earth? Why are you here? Why did God send you to the particular ministry that you're in? Why are you in the body of Christ? Why are you saved? You need to ask yourself these questions. Then make a decision about what you are going to do about why you are here to achieve.

We can preach people into oblivion—a frenzy. Yet those are simple questions that they need to ask in order to live when they stop shouting and go home. What are you here for? What's your purpose for being saved? What is it that God called you to do? Do you know what it is without a shadow of a doubt? What time is it? It's end-time. It's harvest time. This is not the time to live without awareness of your purpose; you have to know why you are here. What was it that you were born to do? Begin to seek God and ask God, how do I get there? How do I do this thing? Show me Lord, how. And if you already know what you're supposed to be doing, then ask God to show you how to get there and do this.

KNOW YOUR PREDESTINED ASSIGNMENT

In Christendom, too many of us don't know what we are supposed to do. We don't know why we were born. Some people say, well I was a mistake or whatever. You know I'm just here, but it's more to you than just being here. You are an extension of the plan and purpose of God from the foundation. You are an extension of the Lord Jesus Christ—an extension of God himself, the Creator of the Universe. You were created and made just like him, in his image. Therefore, there is a divine purpose for you being in the earth realm.

So I say to you, find out what it is that you were born to do and get into it. Put your foot in there and begin to pursue your Destiny! How powerful and overcoming it will be when everybody begins to pursue, begin to walk and begin to process toward his or her Destiny. However, the irony is we can't get out of the process because we're still hanging out in Gilgal. Or we're still in Bethel. Or we're still in Jericho fighting with Satan. We have not overcome yet. We haven't crossed the *Jordan* (*a spiritual situation*) yet. God wants you to get cross Jordan and prevail.

God doesn't want us to be a liability in the church. He doesn't want us to be self-focused and self-centered, where everything revolves around 'me'. It's time now to understand that this is not about you. So if you're mad, if you're heartbroken, if you're rejected and dejected, or offended, you need to realize that it's not about you. It's about the Kingdom. So get over it! This is a hard word and I know it, but the Lord wants me to say this. It's time to experience a real God breakthrough and a real God breakout. I mean a serious breakthrough. I'm not talking about goose bumps stuff. I'm talking about real transformation! I'm talking about a real change!

THE CYRUS ANOINTING

So we need to begin to ask the question: God, what am I here for? Why did you send me to this particular church? What is my purpose in this church? Find out what your purpose is in the church. Some people are scaffoldings. Some people are pillars. Some people are intended to be there forever to help hold up the work until Jesus comes. Those people who are scaffolding, they come just to help build. They come for a season that the man or woman of God is in to help build and then they are gone. So what are you? Are you a pillar or are you scaffolding? Are you in your church to support and help build? You need to find out whether you're scaffolding or a pillar. Wherefore, if you are a pillar, then you need to get into position and begin to support.

Now is the time to get in your position and hold up your part because until you do that part is going to be lacking. If you're scaffolding start getting yourself into position to help hold up and build whatever area of the church that needs to be built. That is wherever you can edify, encourage and build up. For, if you're not building up, you're tearing down. It is time for us to be builders in God's kingdom—a Cyrus anointing. You cannot be defeated! You are a person of success. God has dropped success in your belly. He would not send you to a ministry, to a man or woman of God who has success in them without predestining you for success.

When you plant (*invest time, talent, resources*) into a church, you get everything that's in that leadership. It comes to you. That's why it is not good to be wanderers because when you're a wanderer you're not established in good soil where you can grow. You don't get anything. You can't really get the complete, full potential of a ministry—everything comes from the head down. For example, when the brain ceases to function the whole body stops. It is akin to when you let the spiritual leader get damaged, the whole body suffers. So, you must build up and *strengthen* the head, and don't let someone talk against your leadership. This is where you got to get apostolic boldness, put your hand up and say, "No, you will not say that about our leadership. They may not be perfect, but you will not say that, and I rebuke it in the name of Jesus."

The Lord is no longer going to pacify the church. God is not giving us baby talk and a pacifier. We've got enough word in us now to go on to heaven. We don't need more word. We got enough to go to heaven. But we need to take the word that's in us, begin to activate it and put it to work. Begin to utilize that word and start building. You are a builder. You have the strength inside of you. God said he has given you a new level of strength. He's given you a might in your inner man that's not by power, nor by might but by His Spirit. He's putting a new might, a new strength, a new power and boldness inside of you now to finish the work, to do what God has ordained you to do in your ministry.

God has plans for the ministry where you hold membership; the plans of God are embedded in wealth, because there is treasure in the ministry. The adversary will deploy the personalities of Sanballat and Tobiah to literally try to stop the work. But they can't get a foothold in a church that has a strong level of prayer, a robust level of worship, effective teaching, and order within its organization. The enemy is blocked more easily when these components are operational within a ministry and the opposite is evident when it is not.

TREASURE WHERE YOU ARE

God is speaking to us about moving on and advancing the kingdom. As the body of Christ, we're all in a process and are coming through this thing. We're all processing to something. What are we transforming into? Where is God leading us? He's directing us to a destination. There's a Destiny that God has ordained for everyone; you have a Destiny. Before you were in your mother's womb, while you were still in God's heart, God had a plan for you. He had a plan for you to be stationed in your current position for his purpose and plan…so get comfortable with the process and just follow the blueprint.

Ask yourself why are you there? Perhaps you would have left, but you couldn't leave. You're still there. What is it that God has planned for you? There is treasure where you are. God is getting ready to release abundance, greatness, influence and favor in the church. It's not just "my grace is sufficient" but favor is getting stuff that nobody else is getting: getting positions, jobs and promotions when no-one else is. That's what favor is—when everything else around you is dry and barren, you are flourishing. Everything is moist (full of life) and you're being blessed!

When all hell is breaking out around you and everybody else is gasping for relief, God's got you cloaked in where nothing touches you. There is a season that God will cause you to come to a rest. That's favor where nothing is touching you. For instance, when others around you are getting terrible flu viruses as well as other illnesses, and you know that your immune system isn't as strong as it should be but you are physically well. You don't get sick. That's nothing but favor.

When you go to the hospital and the doctors give you a bad diagnosis, they give you up because of what's happening to you and you should be dead, but you can't die, that's favor—you are walking in God's favor. When your head should have exploded, God said no. God said, "you shall live and not die and declare the works of the Lord!" God is gracing you to live in this season. He said, *"I'm gracing you with life in this season because it's not over yet and I'm going to give you strength in your body to do what I have called you to do. You will rise again to an empowered dimension."* God's going to bring you beyond where you were. Just say I'll rise again! No power on earth can hold me down. Nothing can stop me now. God has put a defense around you. Praise the Lord we got a defense!

We got angels watching over us. Nothing can touch us that the Father doesn't want to touch us. When the enemy comes in like a flood, the Spirit of God will lift up a standard. When the enemy comes—the Spirit will come like a flood! Don't you doubt God now! For every hint of doubt that's trying to harass you right now, you tell the devil: I'm under the Cyrus Anointing and I am a Warrior in the Spirit. I'm powerful in the Holy Ghost! You got to let the devil know I'm not afraid of you! I'm not taking anything off you. Cancer I'm not afraid of you! What you fear will come upon you, but even if it comes, God will put you in a supernatural place of peace—a place where it can't take or hold on to your peace. The storm will stop, and your peace will remain.

Double Lifestyle

So God is getting us ready for the greatest season of Christendom. We're embarking upon the final stages of the present conditions of this earth realm. The church is being prepared. The glory is about to cover the earth. He is talking about the church. He is talking about us. We are the glory of the Lord to be revealed. So we must begin to purify, wash and cleanse ourselves. We must begin to walk in obedience to God. Walk in a new level of holiness. Walk in a new level of purification, a new level of honesty with a new attitude.

I taught a lesson at our church on Attitude because people in the body of Christ have a tendency to be Dr. Jekyll and Mr. Hyde. We're living a double life, but God is dealing with that double lifestyle where we are one thing in the church and we're something else when we go home. We are angels in church—that is to pretend we live godly in church, but when we get home, we are vicious devils—a person can't even live with some Christians.

Nevertheless, God is processing us, so if you're in that place don't lose hope because God is still working it out in you. You are going to come out of it. You're coming through it. Don't worry. It's just a matter of adjustment. God's adjusting you. That's right, you're getting readjusted. God is putting a new anointing on you to build you up. God is restoring you. He is taking away some old practices and putting a new realm of conscience that will empower you to life infused with power. You may be in what seems like a crazy place right now, but it is just a holding pattern. We're in the position for takeoff. You haven't seen the finished work yet.

We're processing on this journey and coming out of these hard places where God is establishing us for Kingdom dominion. He's working everything out that's not like him. He is just working the hell out of us really. Yes, he's taking hell out of us. He's trying to get heaven in us and hell out of us. This is serious business. You got too many hellions in the church. God's trying to work heaven in us, so that we can start getting along with one another—so that we can work together as a team and get unified.

GOD'S CLEANING HOUSE

The reason why we are not unified is because the enemy is too busy in some of our lives. However, God is giving you victory over that one that's been your enemy, heckling you and keeping you frustrated. I don't care if it's in your house or folks in the church struggling with you—people frustrating you causing you anxiety and stress. God wants you to get beyond that in your spirit so that your growth isn't impaired. So that your feelings aren't always hurt by remembrance of the deeds.

Many Christians are governed too much by what they feel—For instance, I feel like she doesn't like me. I feel rejected. I feel hurt. I feel offended. See that's the problem. You're feeling too much. That means you're living out of your *soulish* realm and allowing external factors to control your walk. When people talk like that to me, I say oh, I know they're in trouble now because they're saying, I feel like God wants me to leave my church. On the other hand, I feel like Gods telling me…Wait a minute! If God is telling you to leave the ministry, then your leadership ought to know it. If it's time for you to go, your leadership ought to be the first one to know that God is sending you out. In fact, in an Apostolic church people shouldn't just get up and walk out. I believe the leaders are supposed to send them out.

This is a hard teaching. You can't sugarcoat in this hour. You can't pet people up and preach them under the pews because when they get through, they go home and they're still not transformed. People need some good down to earth teaching. When I speak at conferences, I don't try to entertain folks, but I teach women about how they ought to live. I tell women today how they ought to keep their home, and how to take care of their husbands and they're children.

I tell women "listen, you can't prophesy anything to me if your house is dirty. Don't you prophesy one word to me if your house is torn apart! Can't even find your bed! More dishes in the sink than there are in the cabinets and you think that you can prophesy to me? You have nothing to tell me. Clean your house!" This is the kind of stuff that need to be taught in this hour because of the disorder in the church; many evangelists and ministers aren't accountable to anyone and seek to establish their own kingdom. One's gift/talent isn't more significant to God than relationship ... God's desire for those in leadership is to teach his children how to be intimate with him, to love him, and share that knowledge with the next one.

Let's clean up and put first things first.

Well, I work too you say. That's good if you work too. It's also beneficial if the man of the house participates in the process of keeping the house; it should be a joint effort.

Help her.

When we hear basic things like this, we think they are not good but they are. We think they are not connected to that which is spiritual, yet they are. I preached a message like this in Washington, D.C., and a couple of years later in Nashville, at Judy Jacobs Institute, where a young Caucasian woman came up to me and said "*Mother Nichols, I just want to tell you that I went home, and I cleaned my house. Everything that you told me to do, I did it and God started speaking to me. I started feeling God's anointing on my life increase.*"

God is not going to speak to you in a nasty house! God spoke to a woman in a church in Grand Rapids; she was trying to pray and touch

God for the needs in her life. She kept feeling an *uncertain* presence in her house and part of it was demonic. She started feeling another presence—an angel manifested in her home and told her 'clean this house up! God said I will not dwell in a dirty house!' An angel from heaven came and told her clean your house up! You might not like it, but it's spiritual. It's about kingdom order. You know I hear God more clearly and get some of my greatest messages when I'm pushing a vacuum sweeper. You need to know the advantages of being a housewife. There is a *delicate* power in being a housewife!

SPIRITUAL MOTHERS IN ZION

At conferences, I've talked to the women about Deborah and Jael. Deborah, in the Old Testament, was a judge in Israel that accompanied Barak and Israel's army to battle at his request. When the opposition began losing, Sisera, the head of the opposing army ran and went for cover into the tent of a woman name Jael. Jael, a housewife, was working in the house and that woman, that housewife with a cup of milk and a steak knife, worked him over! What an *entire* army couldn't do, a housewife did! She got the strong man. A housewife can get the strong man! You got to know how to work your stuff. You got to know how to work what you got up in your house. Clean your house!

Don't let that man come home from work to find a cold piece of bologna! You've been in the house all day, and he's been at work all day and he comes home from work to a cold piece of bologna. The devil is a liar! When my husband used to work, he never came home from work (not one-day) without a hot meal waiting for him and his bath water already prepared when he got there. That's why I can teach this because I've walked it. If anybody knows me, they know that I'm an immaculate housekeeper. You're not going to find anything out of place in my house. I have a tendency to overdo it.

So this teaching may pertain to the natural, but it's spiritual too. After you get through buck-dancing, jumping and running around the church and speaking in tongues, and laying hands on folk and prophesying, you still got to go home and handle business. If your household, your wife or your husband is not happy, don't prophesy.

Bring order to your home first – induce some happiness in the lives of those with whom you dwell then offer the world your anointed gift. Your first ministry is always where you live, not where you work or attend church.

Furthermore, we are going to be a powerful people when we take care of our homes first. The church won't be any greater than your home. A lot of the disorder at the church has to do with what's going on at home. Shine the light! Some of us just need to make a decision to do what is right at home. You will be surprised at the anointing that will be released on your life when you handle business the right way. God wants order.

That's why it's hard for the man or woman of God to get order in the church. When your household is not in order, everything else is out of order. Everybody's confused. The wife doesn't know who she is. The husband doesn't know who he is. Everybody's trading places. It's the truth. It's time for us now to get in position because God's getting ready to release some stuff. We're getting ready to come into our greatness. There's a new level of power coming if you go home clean that refrigerator out, get them clothes out that's been stacked up in that closet for six weeks. You can't even put your shoes in there because you got dirty clothes all over the closet. Take some of that stuff and give it away. You're hoarding up a whole lot of stuff. Hoarding says something about what is in your spirit. The more junk there is in your house, the more junk in your spirit. If your house is confused, there is a sign that a spirit of confusion is on you.

You may think this is hard, but I love you enough to tell you the truth. These are the kinds of words now that's going to cause us to come to life in this hour. It's not all about the tongue speaking because you can speak in tongues in church, go home, and curse somebody out. You can go home and fuss like two worlds coming to an end and then want to come and prophesy. I don't think so! Let's get things right in the *family*, then we can come together in unity in the church.

I don't want to leave you on a negative note, so brothers get in there and help your wife clean the house so you all can hear clearly from God and see clearly. Get a new attitude. Get a new focus and you'll be able to discern. Your discernment gets sharper after you clean up. Then you can see just where the devil is. You see the devil likes to hang out in the mess. He likes confusion. He hangs out where the dirt is. You got garbage all over the place and stuff, shoes, and boots all in the corner. You got light bulbs burnt out and darkness in the house. The devil loves that. Put bulbs up in that house! Get those dark corners out of that house!

I've said many things and I pray that your ears were open to hear what the spirit of the Lord is saying. You must receive by faith into your spirit, in order to birth forth everything you've been ordained to birth forth in this season. This is a walk of faith. This prayer journey is a journey of faith. So as we proceed on this prayer journey, as we keep our eyes fixed and focused on God, he will cause us to receive all the inheritance that belongs to us.

Restoration, reformation and the eradication of confusion in our houses and then our spirit man! Clean the physical house and the spiritual house. First the natural then spiritual! When we begin to tap into the natural, (those things we can see) then God will cause our spirits to begin to change and be transformed. And if you're in that place where you need to get things in order be encouraged you shall prevail. This is a place where ministry is born.

The gift of ministry that God has placed in your belly is also purified. The gift is released and you can do entirely what God has predestined for you to do as you allow God's healing waters to flow out of your belly healing you physically and emotionally to the core of your battle—delivered! You can break through the struggle and continue to rise in God, where we go from glory-to-glory and now walk as a mature son of God, totally delivered and healed. That's what the process and the struggle is all about. That's why God placed a dream seed of purpose in you from the foundation while you were yet in your mother's womb. This is what the struggle in the church has been about, a struggle between wheat and tares whether they be intrinsic or extrinsic. This is what the fourth level of the prayer journey and crossing over Jordan is all about.

This information is so important that it bears repeating: Jordan is a place of death and separation. You must spend time with God in prayer. You must die daily—put this flesh under daily—death and separation from your flesh, from your carnal nature, from your desires; your own opinions, your own ideas; from every religious spirit and every negative attitude. For after you experience this death and separation, God will step in and says I'm going to reward you. Ask me for anything! This summarizes Section III, the Prayer Journey ends with the Fourth Level— the first crossing of Jordan.

However, there is another level of Jordan that supersedes the Fourth level—the first crossing which I've termed here as "The Second

Crossing of Jordan" where you overcome, get the victory and obtain power with God. Jordan leads you to that final destination, that place of reward. In the pages that follow, we shall study this place in God. Another dimension! A dimension of victory, where power with God, obtains you a Double Portion of the Anointing! So let's continue with that place of reward at Jordan, the second crossing—The Fifth dimension!

REFLECTION AND STUDY QUESTIONS

1. Are you a born-again believer abiding in a church under the fellowship and covering of a spiritual authority? Do you know the vision of the house and can state the vision in words? Write the vision of the house in your own words.

2. What is your part in the corporate assignment? Are you scaffolding? If so, what is it you're supposed to be doing?

3. What hindrances do you encounter? And how can you overcome them?

4. Are you a pillar? Are you doing what you're supposed to be doing? If not, what interference and obstacles are you encountering? How can you get the victory in that area?

9. Define a double lifestyle; Does your definition line up with the Bible?

10. Are you still fantasizing over what could have been? Or have you discovered the treasure where you are?

12. Is your house in order? Could you invite Jesus to live there for a week with you and the family? Think about what he would see and hear. Does it line up with what he would expect of his disciples?

13. What treasures are located right where you are?

SECTION V

THE FIFTH DIMENSION:

NOW IS YOUR TIME!

In 2nd Kings the second chapter we read that the sons of the prophets were at Jericho while Elijah and Elisha had crossed over Jordan. Here, they had processed into a place where they had clout and favor with God. So now they could ask. When you are anointed with favor, you can ask God for anything you want. So here is where Elijah asked Elisha, what shall I do for you before I am taken away from you? Elisha said, "I pray you, let a double portion of your spirit be upon me"; a double portion of your anointing, your ability—the thing that you walked in. Elijah is now teaching Elisha a final lesson before he took his flight.

Accordingly, as we, your leaders, begin to ascend into new places in the spirit (when we come up out of a place and leave a place in the spirit) we drop that mantle of the old. It's an old mantle for us, but it's new for you. The particular aspect about this process is there's a double anointing that goes with it. Though it was Elijah's old mantle, it was a new mantle for Elisha. He had already released a double portion anointing on it.

What you get from your leadership is double; the impartation from your mentor doubly blesses you that is why you must stay connected because you want the double portion. You won't settle for anything less than the double portion and you say now that I'm in a place where I can ask for what I want, I'm going to ask for double. You just need to get big and bold and say I want double!

You got to know what it is that you want. So what is it that you want from your leaders? What is it that you're going to get from them? When I was on TBN, I said "you don't have to like your mentor to get what you need." Your main objective is to get what's in that leadership whether you understand them or not, whether they appeal to you or not. God sent you to get something and you have to say I'm going to get it! You got to make that determination that I'm going to get what's in the belly of my mentor.

WATCHMAN ON THE WALL

So as they proceeded Elisha said, "Give me a double portion of your spirit." And he said, 'you have asked a hard thing. However, if you see me' (You got to be in position, and you got to be focused.) You got to see! There is an inheritance that you want from your leaders, your spiritual Father and Mother. There is an inheritance that is yours and no-one else can have what rightfully belongs to you. There's something that you have to give him or her that no one else can give them.

They can preach like Peter and swing from the chandeliers. They can break the word down, use Hermeneutics and all that, Exegesis and everything they want to do, but there's something in your leadership that they can't give you; nobody else can give you either. So you might as well get it together and walk with a determined mind that there's something in my spiritual authority, my spiritual leadership that I'm after and I'm going to get it because it's my inheritance! Your spiritual inheritance is the result of your breakthrough, overcoming and getting the victory whereby we are propelled into another dimension of power.

INTIMACY - THE FINAL FRONTIER

The end of Elijah's journey at Jordan brought him to full power and into the presence of the glory of God. I call that place, intimacy; where he became one with God. That's what he was trying to teach Elisha intimacy, becoming one with God. There is a place; there is an end to this journey. There's a final end to all this hell you're going through. The end of it, where you are processing to is that oneness with God, unity with God where you can have favor with God. You can speak a thing and see it come to pass! You and God become one, and deeply intertwined; God in you and you in him, call it the inner court. We must journey through the different levels of prayer to release God's greater glory and his divine favor and power in our lives.

Intimacy is the final frontier. It is where the believer and God become one, intertwined. Most of Christendom, haven't reached that yet because we're still too controlled by outward circumstances. We're still moved and influenced by things going on around us. That's how you know that you're not intimate with God. When you get to that place where you and God are one together outside influences don't affect you. When you are intertwined with God, outside influences are subdued.

I saw my mother come to that place where outside things didn't influence her. She came to a place that nothing bothered her anymore. She finally reached it. She had come to the final frontier of her journey. That didn't mean she was getting ready to die; but it meant that she had found that place she had sought from God. She had processed and went through hell; but she determined I am going to get this thing. She had sought her God and found him because her endeavor was to know him.

What it means to know him is to be intimate with him, to know him in the power of his resurrection and the fellowship of his suffering. Jesus had that relationship with his Father. He knew his Father. He had oneness with his Father. He was God and God was him; yet, he was all man. Still God dwelt in him, and he resided in God, and they were one. God wants to bring the church into that oneness with him, intertwined.

ANOINTING OF FAVOR

The final portion of this lesson begins with verse eleven: "As they still went on and talked, behold a chariot of fire and horses of fire parted the two of them, and Elijah went up by a whirlwind into heaven. And Elisha saw it and he cried my father, my father!" He recognized him (if at no other time) he recognized at that time the identity of this man whom he had served all these years. That's why you got to stay in position so that you can be anointed to see clearly. So, Elisha recognized him, and he said, my Father. His eyes were fixed and set on this man because this man had in him what he desired, and what he had been longing for and what he had been serving for. Your serving is not in vain, as you serve in the ministry. You get your inheritance through serving.

In verse twelve it says "and Elisha saw it and he cried, my father, my father! The chariot of Israel and its horsemen! And he saw him no more. And he took hold of his own clothes and tore them in two pieces." He took off his old garments. Everything that Elisha was, everything that he thought he was, all of his preconceived notions, his own opinions and ideas he took them off. Here it is now he's at this place and this position. He processed through every phase and now he sees himself. He sees that I can't go where I'm going; I can't follow in the footsteps of my mentor with these clothes on so he rent his clothes in half. He separated himself from his old.

You got to separate yourself from the old. You can't take old attitudes, old ideas, old concepts and old pre-conceived notions into this new place that God is taking you. Where God is getting ready to take you, you have to take off them old clothes. You can't take this old anointing into the new place that God is taking you because it's requiring a new anointing. I keep hearing God say it's an anointing of favor. That dropped in my spirit and you better catch that! There's an anointing of favor. So Elisha tore his clothes. He took off the old and he put on the new. He took off his old clothes and he took up the mantle of Elijah— Elijah's cloak that fell from him and he threw it around himself and went back and stood by the bank of the Jordan (the place where he had crossed over with his father), where he had the anointing and the favor of God on him to ask for whatsoever he desired.

THE ANOINTING TO STAND

So he took his father's mantle, he goes back and looks at what happens in verse fourteen: "And he took the mantle that fell from Elijah and struck the waters and said, where is the Lord, the God of Elijah? And when he had struck the waters, they parted this way and that and Elisha went over." Take note: The first time Elisha came over with his father. The second time Elisha came over, he went back by himself. Elijah was trying to teach him how to stand with God alone. You cannot depend on people. You need the anointing to stand in this hour. This is a revelation somebody needs to hear so I'll say it again, "You need the ANOINTING to stand!"

This is a new journey that you are getting ready to embark upon, and on this new journey, you won't be able to take your brother, your sister, your mama or your papa. You won't be able to take Susie, Sally or Joe because we are coming into that place where everybody is going to have to stand on his or her own now. You are going to have to make a decision to separate yourself. You may not like that because you're trying to take everybody with you and not everybody is going where you are going. Not everybody is going to buy into the vision. Not everybody knows what is in you. Not everyone is going to celebrate you!

Therefore, he went back across the Jordan. He struck that water and said, "Where is the God of Elijah? I want to meet with him." Isn't it strange that he would say that after having crossed with his spiritual father but evidently, he wasn't paying attention. He had something else going on. He was thinking about getting that mantle. So, he said where is the God of Elijah? And when he struck the water, the waters parted for him and he went across alone.

You are going to cross over! You got to get a new attitude. You need a mega shift in your mindset. It may not be common or normal; it is a hard thing, but you got to strip yourself from old seasonal mindsets. You got to change your thinking. You must change this stinking thinking and stop trying to take everybody with you. Those that will go, they will go and those that won't, they won't. This is where the rubber meets the road. Many that you try to take with you will discredit the power and the anointing on your life. They'll discredit the gift in you. They'll try to discredit the influence that you have.

DESTINY TO FULFILL

So Elisha went back across alone and he didn't have any fear going across because he had come across previously with his father. He went back because he had a destiny to fulfill! When he crossed over the Jordan, he struck the waters and they parted. In addition, when the sons of the prophets who were watching at Jericho saw him they said, "The spirit of Elijah rests on Elisha."

You see God will let somebody announce your anointing. Now here they identify him. This is important, so let me say that again, God will cause somebody to see you and they will announce your anointing. You do not have to tell anybody who you are because God will let somebody announce you to the world! People will see what's in you and they will say, 'That's a prophet. That's an Apostle. That's a Teacher. That's a Pastor'—they will validate your office. Yes, God will divinely direct your coming out party; he promised to spread a table before you in the presence of your enemies… he kept them close enough just so that they could witness your ascension to new dimensions. So the ones who had been heckling him, now see him standing on his own and they have to concede that the God of Elijah is with him, bows, and says, "Oh he's a different person. Oh, he is not the same. I see the spirit of Elijah on him." When others are watching you, you got to keep going.

You cannot stop to listen to distractive voices that are saying, "Your head is going to die today." He's not dead, he went to another dimension! He has been translated and transformed to another dimension; forever changed; forever altered. There is no going back only moving forward with God; it is all or nothing. You got to change your methodology to obtain the things which you see in the spirit realm—the future. Many distractions and detours come to keep you from moving forward, to cause you to lose momentum and to halt progression. However, just because you're going through hell, doesn't mean that God can't work through as a conduit of change and power. When Elisha got to his destination, the supernatural stepped in! The battle was over! He asked and crossed over into the supernatural.

In summary, the four levels of the Prayer journey are Gilgal, Bethel, Jericho, and Jordan. The second crossing or coming back over

Jordan reveals a fifth-degree or fifth dimension where clout with God is obtained. That place with God where you can walk in a jurisdiction of dominion—that you can speak a thing. You can speak a word and say as Elijah said. He didn't say God said. Elijah said, "I SAY it won't rain!" That's the level that God is processing us to where we too can say, "I SAY!" That's power with God.

Nothing unclean, nothing unholy, and overt carnality that we see so often in the body of Christ can reach this dimension. You have to take off the old and when you take off the old, you'll eradicate jealousy, envy, backbiting, lying, manipulation, strife, a proud look and everything else that's not like God. No carnal deeds can dwell in the presence of the Lord in this dimension that's why we must go through the process and go from glory to glory.

Elijah's mantle represents power, a healing balm that would flow out to the nations. The coat of many colors represents the nations. So that coat of many colors as well as my mother's mantle that I wore is a part of who I am, and has been a part of the process, a part of who I'm to become. My final destination of which gifts and callings have been utilized in the kingdom of God to accomplish some things, to bless the lives of His people, as well as my own. One of the manifested outpourings of that mantle occurred in Chicago mentioned in section two. That was only the beginning. God is returning—He's restoring!

He is restoring my ministry! I am coming full circle in my work. That's why I shared with you about how God used me in such a powerful way in Chicago. God used me so that it was turning Chicago upside down! I am once again positioned to supernatural alter the path that many are walking to bring healing, wealth, peace and a deeper understanding of who they are in Christ. This is an exciting moment in my life.

To witness the tangible manifestation of what I birthed in my spirit was awesome; it was such a powerful time to experience God— Elijah's mantle—The Elijah to Elisha conference!

This conference in 2005 some twelve years later was a significant, pivotal fork in the road. The number twelve has a specific prophetic meaning in God: divine government, apostolic government.[1] That conference was prophetically named *Elijah-to-Elisha* where the prophecy unfolded: Jacob is running from his past defeats, overcomes, gets the victory and obtains power with God. Elisha overcomes; he made it through the demanding process and obtained the mantle. Likewise, I processed to another level where God said I was now ready to wear my mother's mantle. That is why it is important for us to prevail, to get the victory and to overcome so we can have power with God and obtain favor with men.

---

[1] From 'Dream Language' by James W. and Michal A. Goll

THE PROPHECY UNFOLDS: ONE NIGHT WITH THE KING

I began this book with a dream because God starts with dreamers. He plants seeds in to our hearts through prophecy and then he brings us full circle through the process of purification. A part of that dream wasn't shared, but I will now. In 2005, God told me one Saturday: He said, "The Scepter is in this church just like he gave it to Esther for such a time as this. He said I placed the Scepter in your hand. And Haman can't stop what God is doing because God has raised up a Mordecai. Mordecai is on assignment in your life. The Holy Ghost is your Mordecai and he's watching over your assignment."

All you have to do now that you've crossed over is say to God: Bid me to come! (What do you want?) Bid me to come. They told Esther you can't go in there before time. Esther said don't worry I've already been through my season of preparation. I completed my process. And now that we've been through the process, we can cry tears of joy rather than tears of sadness. Now that you've been through the process and season of preparation, having suffered, your season changed and now consists of myrrh and frankincense; a season of sweet smelling perfume. The kingdom of God includes a citywide revival and the aroma goes all over the city. The sweet-smelling savor is going all over the city. The aroma is coming out of the walls and everywhere you go, you leave the aroma of God's glory.

What is the scepter? The scepter is authority and God has released it in this house. God has released the authority and with that authority comes responsibility. He also released keys and keys represent authority. As a result, Esther said, "Bid me to come!" She said, "If I perish, I perish, but I'm going to see the King." That has to be the cry of your heart. That has to be the stance of your mindset. If I perish, I perish, but I'm going in. I'm going all the way, all the way into the throne to the Fifth Dimension. So daughter of destiny go through the process. Son of God ascend to the high place in God. Go through your Gilgal; go through Bethel, Jericho and Jordan. All those places are symbolic, but whatever you have to do, do it and finish the course.

Then you can also say like the Apostle Paul, I fought a good fight. I finished my course. I kept the faith. It's already finished. It was finished at the cross on Calvary. You need only to believe, confess it with your mouth, walk it out by faith, activate the word, and move into what God preordained for you from the foundation of the world—your spiritual inheritance! Walk into your Destiny!

EPILOGUE

DIVINE PURPOSE

In conclusion, being a mentor and a spiritual mother, I want to end on a more personal note that deals some more with the family. Even though God separates us from them at a particular season of time, they will always be a part of our legacy. It's all a part of coming full circle. You become what you were predestined to become. You become what God says you are. Now listen! I want to reiterate this: God has already set your course; whether you were born as (what the world calls illegitimately and assumed to be a bastard child). I feel a need to emphasize more here on family dynamics because it is a major stronghold in the life of many believers. You were meant to be on this earth no matter whom your family is, whether your mother and your father, the two people that came together and created you intended for it or not, you were still meant to be here. So, God has a divine plan, a divine purpose for your life for greatness and for success.

Whatever you do, don't consider yourself a failure because of your family and your past upbringing. Perhaps you thought that you never had what you should have had. You may have been dirt poor even as I was, but as I said previously when I spoke to you about having *"treasure,"* there's something very wonderful even in that. You can reflect and you can remember the wonderful things—the good times as well as the bad times. Take the good times, emphasize on them, and let them dominate your life and take the bad times and use them as stepping-stones, as opportunities to change. So that you don't take the path if it was negative that you're parents took; or the path of that one parent or whoever it was that raised you. You don't have to go in that direction. That's a valuable lesson. Those are valuable stepping-stones for you embedded in making a choice.

YOUR WILL –VS- DESTINY

We may not want to hear that word choice again, but that's what it's all about, making a determined choice. God has predestined us, but we're also created in his image with free will. All through our life, we are always confronting our will. There's always going to be a battle between our will and choice. Let me say that there's always a battle between our will and our destiny. It's that struggle. And your will is the power to choose the way that you want to go. God does not take your will from you. When we learn to make the right choices, we arrive sooner, having deflected many pitfalls that the enemy set up to entrap us. However, if you make bad choices, you will have some setbacks, but the process is the same. You still have to go through the process. You might find yourself back in Gilgal, that place of cycling, struggling, and wrestling with "carnal desires," but you will get there.

WHO DO MEN SAY YOU ARE?

So understand your history and this world in the natural sense. Our greatest example is Jesus. In Mark the eighth chapter, he asked the disciples "who do men say that I am?" Jesus knew who he was and who he was predestined and destined to be. However, his question to his disciples asked who did the society—the world says he was? Then he asked who did his followers, his disciples say he was. Peter gave the divine revelation of who Jesus was. The question was a life and death answer.

Your family and the people around you are similar to the followers. They are familiar with you, your strengths as well as your weaknesses. And even though your family can be detrimental to your spiritual health, you may still cling to them because they are familiar. Family-ties, (including friends, acquaintances whoever is familiar with you) are a stronghold that must be broken in the process. Then you have the socio-economic climate of the world that places a definition on you. That stronghold must be broken too. Every ill-conceived notion of men, and every ill-conceived thought about yourself must be broken. That is why it is important to know whom you are in God, to know who God says you are from the foundation of the world.

Therefore, you got to go through the process of life to birth the prophecy spoken. Keep it real on this journey by learning the assignment early on from God that was given from the foundation of the world and walk it out to manifestation. God will take one person that loves him, that is willing and that is not afraid of the devil and turn a city upside down. That's what God wants to do. His call is extended to the pews as well as the pulpit in this hour. He wants to use you to be World changers! Community changers! Atmosphere changers! God is raising up sons and daughter to transform "*nations*" people, to transform cities, to transform the world from the kingdom of men to the kingdom of God. Will you be one?